FEARLESS COMPETITORS

ROLLER DERBY

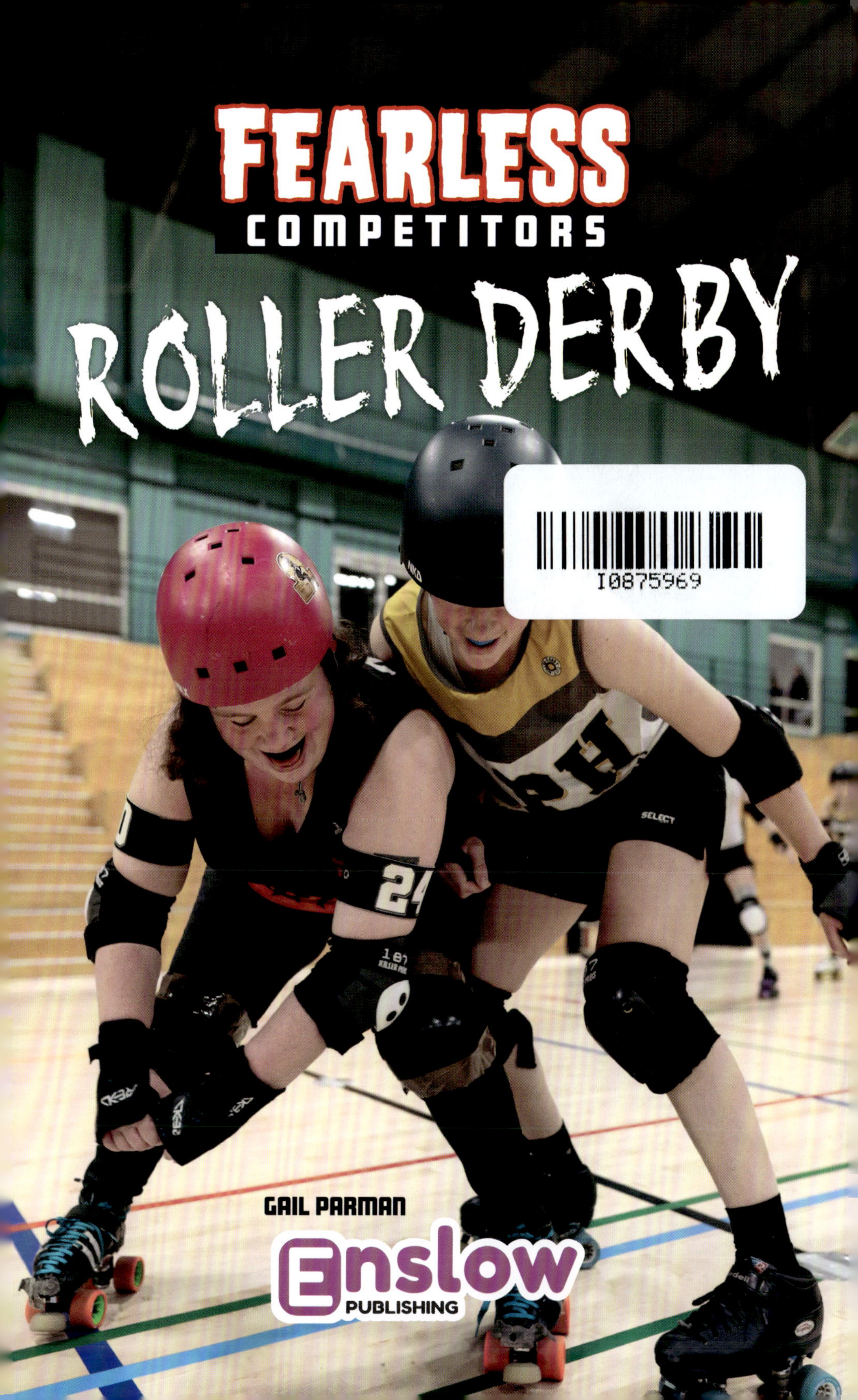

GAIL PARMAN

Enslow PUBLISHING

Please visit our website, www.enslow.com. For a free color catalog of all our high-quality books, call toll free 1-800-398-2504 or fax 1-877-980-4454

Published in 2027 by
Enslow Publishing
2544 Clinton Street
Buffalo, NY 14224

Portions of this work were originally authored by Demi Jackson and published as *Daredevil Sports: Roller Derby.* All new material in this edition is authored by Gail Parman.

Cataloging-in-Publication Data
Names: Parman, Gail.
Title: Roller derby / Gail Parman.
Description: Buffalo, NY : Enslow Publishing, 2027. | Series: Fearless competitors | Includes glossary and index.
Identifiers: ISBN 9781978548930 (pbk.) | ISBN 9781978548947 (library bound) | ISBN 9781978548954 (ebook)
Subjects: LCSH: Roller derby--Juvenile literature.
Classification: LCC GV859.6 P377 2027 | DDC 796.21--dc23

Printed in China

Photos Credits: p. Cover, 1, 14 Beata Janeczko/Shutterstock.com; p. 3 New Africa/ Shutterstock.com; p. 3, 4, 6, 8, 10, 12, 15, 16, 19, 21, 22, 24, 26, 28 (black background) Propakages/Shutterstock.com; p. 4 KennStilger47/Shutterstock.com; p. 6 Susan Montgomery/Shutterstock.com; p. 9, 12 Wikipedia/Shutterstock.com; p. 10 Eurekastreet/ Shutterstock.com; p. 17 joseph donnelly/Shutterstock.com; p. 18 Toasted Pictures/ Shutterstock.com; p. 20 Public Domain; p. 22 Marben/Shutterstock.com; p. 24 Ronald Sumners/Shutterstock.com; p. 26 Trygve Finkelsen/Shutterstock.com; p. 28 Kristina D.C. Hoeppner/Shutterstock.com; p. 30 The Old Major/Shutterstock.com

CPSIA compliance information: Batch #QSENS27: For further information, contact Enslow Publishing, New York, New York, at 1-800-398-2504.

Contents

HIGH SPEED, HARD HITS

You're speeding around the track when an **opponent** comes toward you. You try to skate around her, but she throws her shoulder into your chest. Do you fall, or do you catch yourself and slip past her to score a point? This is roller derby!

FEARLESS FACTS

Roller derby is a full-contact sport. That means skaters can—and do—push, pull, and hit each other!

WHAT IS ROLLER DERBY?

In roller derby, two teams roller-skate around an oval track, trying to score the most points. Each team has five skaters on the track at a time during a game, or bout. Bouts usually last about one hour and are action-packed!

FEARLESS FACTS

Today, roller derby is most popular among women, though there are men's teams and **leagues** as well.

ROLLER DERBY BEGINS

Roller derby started in the 1930s as a roller-skating **event** for entertainment. The crowd loved it when two skaters ran into each other. Soon, the sport changed to make these hits part of it! Roller derby's popularity fizzled out in the 1970s but made a comeback in the 2000s.

FEARLESS FACTS

Early roller derby events took place on banked tracks that were higher along the outside. Today's tracks are flat.

In 2001, a league that formed in Austin, Texas, restarted interest in roller derby, especially among women. Today, there are hundreds of leagues across the United States. Most play on flat tracks. This allows bouts to happen just about anywhere, including at existing roller rinks!

FEARLESS FACTS

Roller derby clubs have taken off in Europe, Australia, and New Zealand as well.

PLAYING THE GAME

Each bout has two 30-minute halves. Within those halves are an unlimited number of jams, or short periods of play. Both teams can score points during the jams, which last up to two minutes or when the lead jammer calls off the jam.

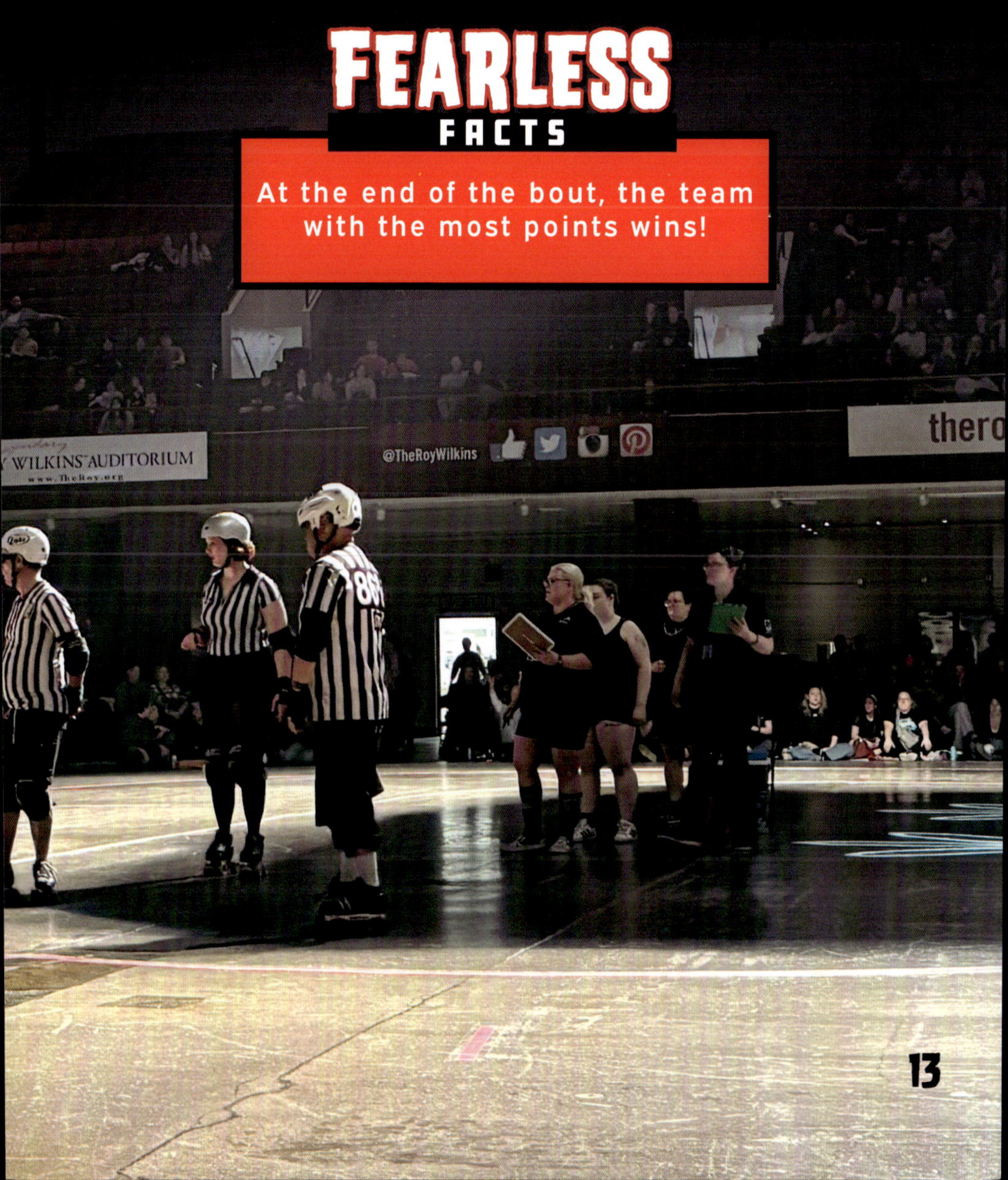

FEARLESS FACTS

At the end of the bout, the team with the most points wins!

Each team has five players on the track at a time: the jammer, blockers, and the pivot. The jammer's job is to score points. Blockers try to stop the other team's jammer and help their jammer through the crowd of skaters. One of the blockers is the pivot, who calls plays and **paces** her team.

FEARLESS FACTS

Jammers wear a helmet cover with a star on it. Pivots wear a helmet cover with stripes. Blockers have a blank helmet.

LET'S PLAY!

At the beginning of a jam, both teams' pivots and blockers line up together behind the start line. They make up the "pack," and the jammers line up behind them. The pack starts to skate at the first whistle. The jammers start once the second whistle sounds.

FEARLESS FACTS

The first jammer to make it through the pack without a **foul** is the lead jammer. She can call off the jam at any time to stop the other team from scoring more points.

23

Jammers score a point for each player of the other team they pass. The blockers play **offense** and **defense** at the same time. They use their bodies to slow or stop the other team's jammer, while helping their own jammer make it through the pack safely.

FEARLESS FACTS

Roller derby has many **referees**. They each have a certain part of the jam to watch, such as counting the lead jammer's points or making sure the blockers are following the rules.

FOLLOW THE RULES

There are many rules in roller derby. There are rules about how skaters can hit each other, how points are scored, and **fouls**. If a player breaks a rule, they are sent to the penalty box for 30 seconds. This leaves their team with one less player on the track.

FEARLESS FACTS

Teams usually have about 15 players total, but only five are on the track at once. Teams can switch skaters between jams.

GEAR UP

Roller derby is fast-paced and full-contact, so safety gear is very important. Each skater needs to wear a helmet that fits well. The best kind for roller derby is plastic with foam inside. Knee pads, wrist guards, elbow pads, and mouth guards are always worn too.

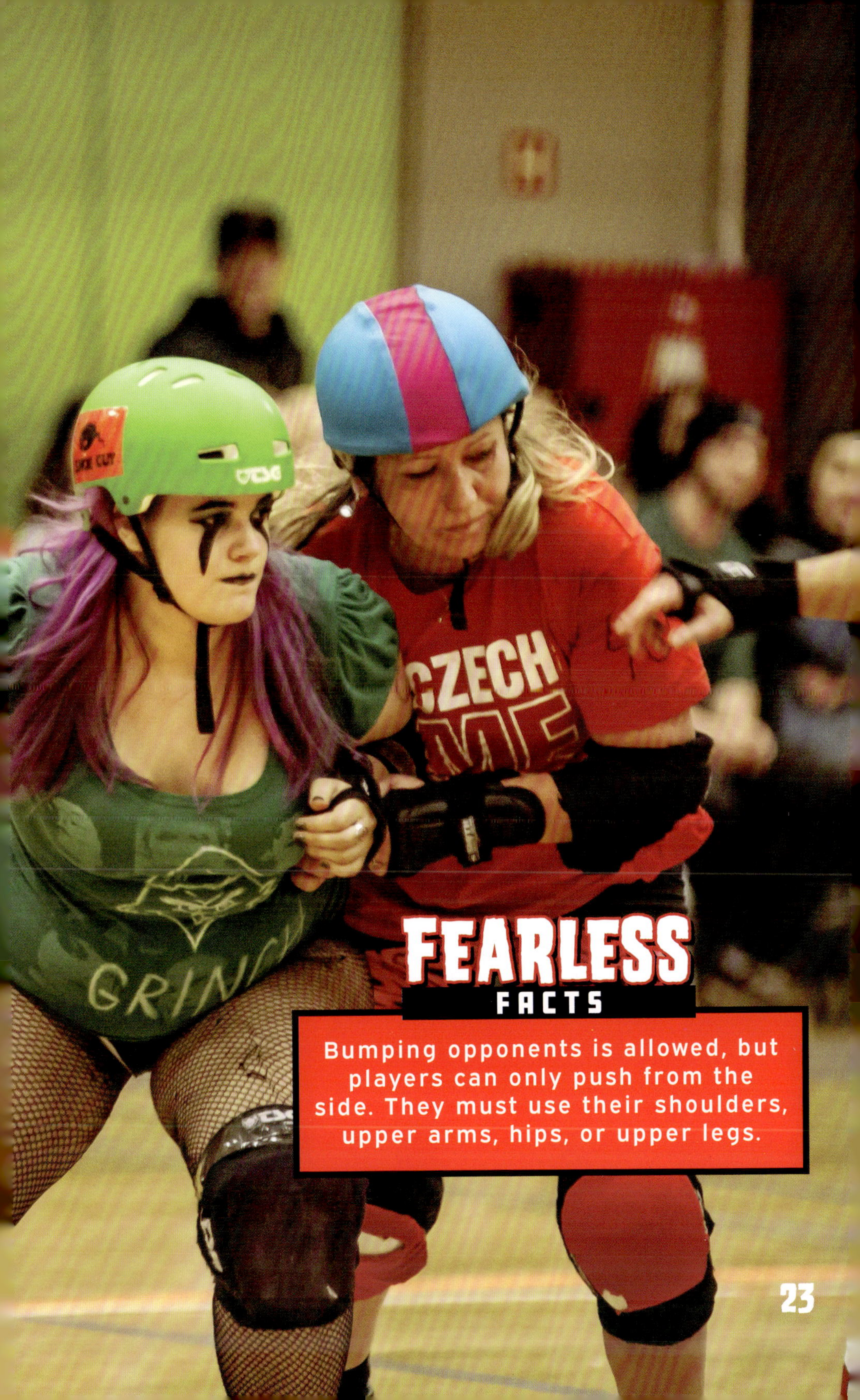

FEARLESS FACTS

Bumping opponents is allowed, but players can only push from the side. They must use their shoulders, upper arms, hips, or upper legs.

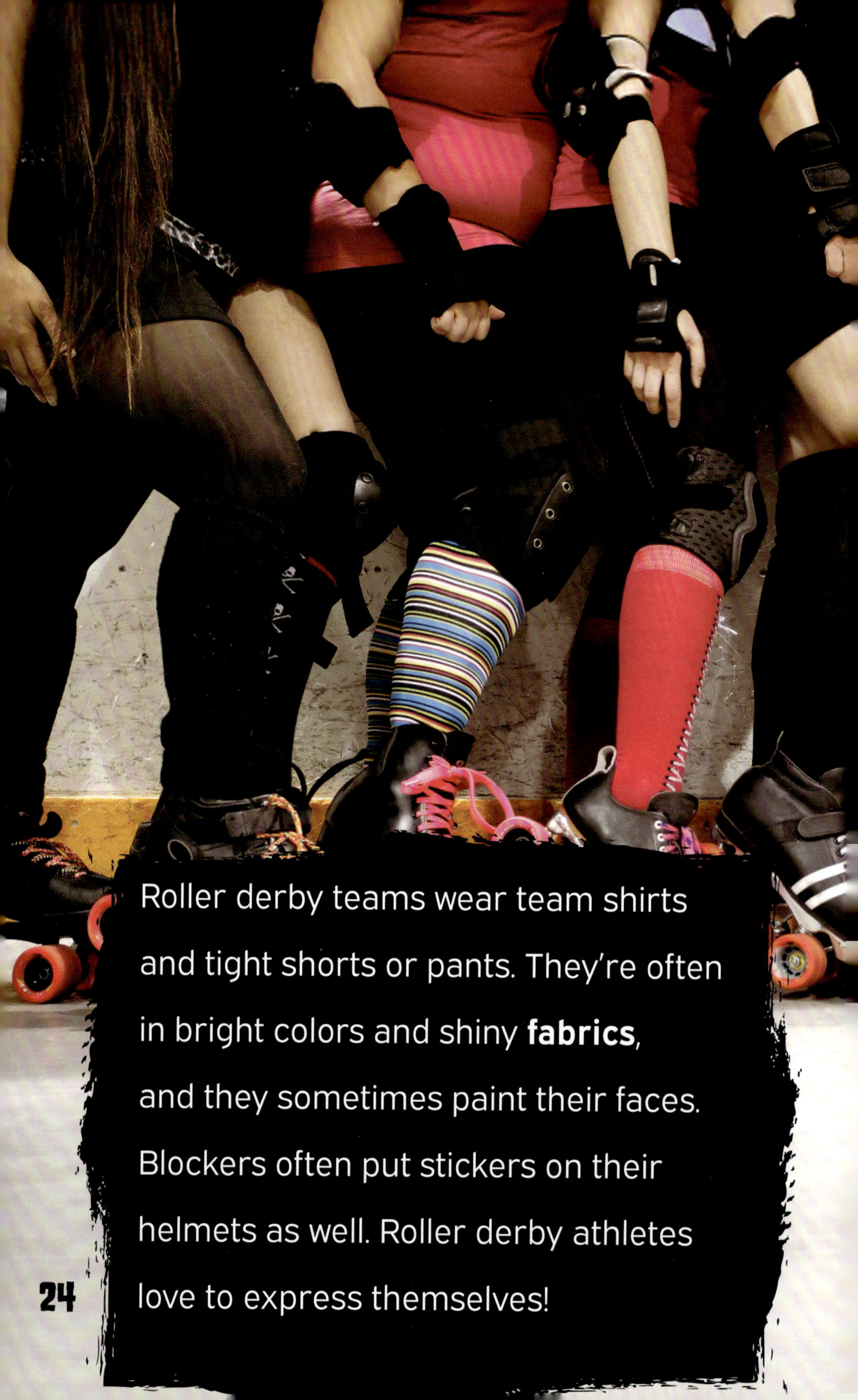

Roller derby teams wear team shirts and tight shorts or pants. They're often in bright colors and shiny **fabrics**, and they sometimes paint their faces. Blockers often put stickers on their helmets as well. Roller derby athletes love to express themselves!

FEARLESS FACTS

Roller derby is a very welcoming sport. Players of all shapes, sizes, and backgrounds can play!

ON FOUR WHEELS

In roller derby, roller skating is important. Athletes need to be able to skate fast and know how to stop and start quickly. They also must be **aggressive** on the track. Perhaps their most important skill is falling safely! Falls happen, even among professionals.

FEARLESS FACTS

Roller derby skaters wear "quad" skates, or roller skates that have four wheels.

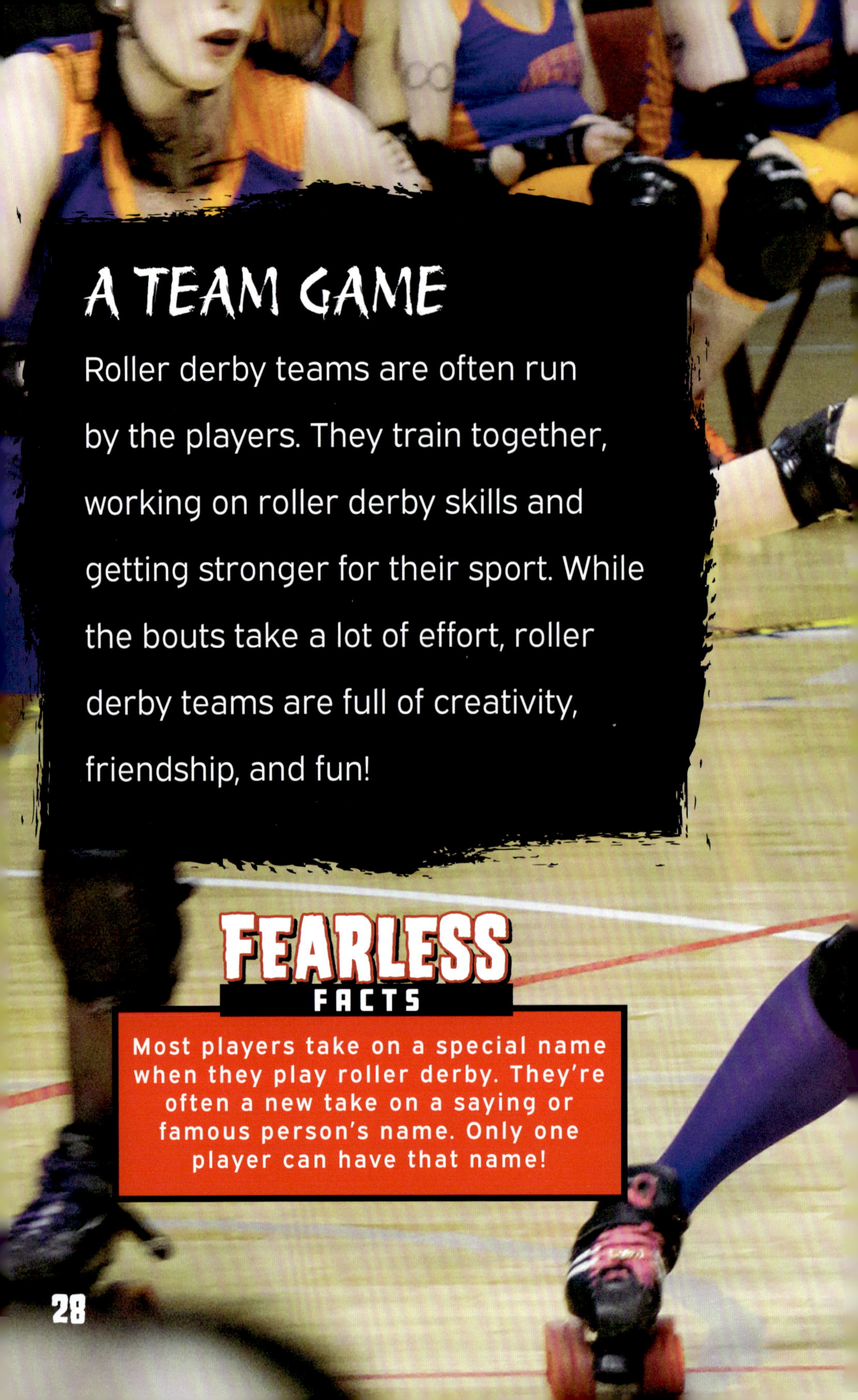

A TEAM GAME

Roller derby teams are often run by the players. They train together, working on roller derby skills and getting stronger for their sport. While the bouts take a lot of effort, roller derby teams are full of creativity, friendship, and fun!

FEARLESS FACTS

Most players take on a special name when they play roller derby. They're often a new take on a saying or famous person's name. Only one player can have that name!

KAISER
SUZI

Safety First

ALL ROLLER DERBY ATHLETES SHOULD:

- wear all proper safety gear, including a helmet, knee pads, elbow pads, wrist guards, and a mouth guard.
- keep skates in good condition.
- stay fit in other ways so they can keep up in a jam.
- take care of any bruises or pain after a practice or bout.
- learn how to fall safely.
- never block other players from behind or use their elbows above shoulder height.

For More Information

BOOKS

London, Martha. *Roller Derby.* SportsZone, 2020.

Marthaler, Jon. *Offbeat Sports.* SportsZone, 2020.

WEBSITES

Junior Roller Derby Association

www.juniorrollerderby.org/

Learn more about roller derby you can try right now!

Welcome to Roller Derby!

https://wftda.com/roller-derby-basics/

Read all about roller derby and watch a short video about the basics of gameplay on the Women's Flat Track Derby Association (WFTDA) website.

Publisher's note to educators and parents: Our editors have carefully reviewed these websites to ensure that they are suitable for students. Many websites change frequently, however, and we cannot guarantee that a site's future contents will continue to meet our high standards of quality and educational value. Be advised that students should be closely supervised whenever they access the Internet.

Glossary

aggressive: acting with forceful energy and purpose

defense: trying to stop the other team from scoring

event: a happening

fabric: a kind of cloth

foul: a breaking of the rules

league: a group of sports teams that face each other

offense: trying to score points

opponent: the person or team you must beat to win a game

pace: to set the speed of

referee: someone who makes sure players follow the rules

Index